# Peanut PROMISES

## Nap 'n' Snack Devotions

Robin Currie

Illustrated by Jack Kershner

CPH.
SAINT LOUIS

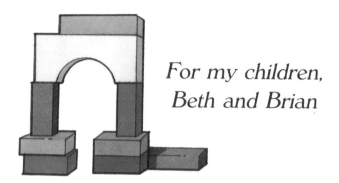

*For my children,*
*Beth and Brian*

Scripture quotations taken from the HOLY BIBLE, NEW INTERNATIONAL VERSION®. NIV®. Copyright © 1973, 1978, 1984 by International Bible Society. Used by permission of Zondervan Publishing House. All rights reserved.

Copyright © 1999 Concordia Publishing House
3558 S. Jefferson Avenue, St. Louis, MO 63118-3968
Manufactured in the United States of America

Library of Congress Cataloging-in-Publication Data

Currie, Robin, 1948–
      Peanut butter promises: nap 'n snack devotions/Robin Currie.
        p.  cm.
      ISBN 0-570-05557-1
      1. Bible stories, English. I. Title.
BS551.2.C875  1999
242 ' .645--dc21

99-19055

1   2   3   4   5   6   7   8   9   10     08   07   06   05   04   03   02   01   00   99

# Contents

# Welcome Home!

## The Story of the Prodigal Son
### (Luke 15:11–24)

Jesus told a story about a man who had two sons.
*Hold up two fingers.*

One day the younger son said to his father, "Give me the money now that you have saved for me."
*Point to self.*

The father gave both of his sons the money he had saved for them. Now they had plenty of money.
*What would you buy with the money?*

The younger son thought it would be fun to go away from home and spend his money. He said good-bye to his father and brother and left home.
*Wave good-bye.*

The younger son walked far away. He spent his money foolishly.
*Shake head no.*

Soon his money was gone. He had no money to buy food or clothes. He was very hungry and very sad.
*Make a sad face.*

The poor boy found a job feeding pigs. The pigs had plenty to eat, but the boy had no good food. He did not like the pig food.
*Make an icky face.*

Then the boy remembered his family.
*Point to head.*

He said, "I'm so hungry. Maybe my father will let me work for him. His workers have plenty to eat."
*Good food—yum! Rub tummy.*

"I will tell my father I'm sorry," the boy decided. "I'm not good enough to be his son."
*Shake head sadly.*

So the son started walking back to his home.
*Pat hands on knees.*

The father saw his son coming down the road and ran to meet him.
*Quickly pat hands on knees.*

He gave his son a big hug.
*Hug yourself.*

The son said, "I'm sorry, Father. I've done many wrong things. I have wasted all your money."
*Make a sad face.*

But the father said, "You are my son. I love you.
I'm happy you are home. We'll have a party to celebrate."
*Make a happy face.*

Jesus told this story to help us learn how much God loves us.
God loves us even when we do things that are wrong.
He helps us say we are sorry.
*Name someone who loves you very much.*

## PRAY TOGETHER BEFORE NAP TIME

Dear God, thank You for my family
who always loves me, no matter
what I do. I know You always
love me too. In Jesus' name.
Amen.

## HAVE FUN TOGETHER AFTER NAP TIME

Build a house with blocks. Make a
long road with blocks or strips of paper.
Make figures of the man and his son
out of chenille wires. Draw bags of
money and pigs and cut them out.
Act out the story. Talk about the joy
the father felt when his son came home.

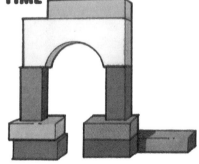

7

The word *prodigal* is sometimes used to refer to a sports star who returns to his first team. Today's society makes us all a bit prodigal. Very few of us live near home, near the place we grew up, near our extended family. Even vacation visits can be stressed and harried as everyone tries to cram a year's worth of loving into one week. Maybe we really can't go home.

The young man in Jesus' parable left home out of defiance, not because of a job transfer. He quickly spent his father's money. After wasting all he was given, he wanted to go home. How would your parents react if you did something so irresponsible? How would you react if your children behaved that way?

How wonderful that God does not judge by our standards! The father in the story did not act as we would, but as our heavenly Father does. He accepted with love the son who was lost and then found, the one who was dead and then alive.

Do you stray from God's love at times? You can go home anytime. God gave the life of His Son to pay for your sins. Your Father is waiting for you with open arms.

## ACTING IN FAITH

Take five minutes to remember something you have done this week that makes you feel ashamed. Watch the scene like a movie in your mind. Picture Jesus standing beside you. Hear Him say, "You are forgiven, even for that. Welcome home! Our Father is waiting."

# Who Will Help?

## The Story of the Good Samaritan

*(Luke 10:30–37)*

Jesus told a story about a man who went on a trip.
He had to walk a long way.
*Pat hands on knees.*

It was dark, and the man was tired.
*Close eyes. It is hard to stay awake.*

Suddenly some bad men jumped out from behind a rock.
*Clap loudly.*

They took the man's money and knocked him down.
Then they ran away.
*Quickly pat hands on knees.*

The man was hurt and needed help. Who would help him?
*Raise palms in a questioning gesture.*

The poor man heard the swish of someone in a robe coming
down the road. Would he help?
*Rub hands together to make a swishing sound.*

No. The swishing robe went by, and the man did not stop.
*Shake head no.*

The man heard footsteps. Someone else was coming.
Would he help?
*Pat hands on knees.*

No. This man did not stop either.
*Shake head no.*

Then the man heard a donkey slowly clip-clopping down the road. It was another traveler. Would he help?

*Pat hands on knees. Say, "Clip clop, clip clop."*

The donkey's feet went slower and slower and slower until ...

*Pat hands on knees. Clip clop, clip clop.*

STOP!

*Clap hands and shout, "Stop!"*

This man did stop to help. He put bandages on the hurt man and gave him water to drink.

*Pretend to take a big drink.*

Then he put the hurt man on his donkey and took him to the next town.

*Shade your eyes and look far away.*

The good helper told an innkeeper to take care of the hurt man until he was better again.

*Smile and nod yes.*

Jesus told this story to help us know that God wants us to help all people who need us.

*Name someone who helps you.*

*Name someone you can help.*

## PRAY TOGETHER BEFORE NAP TIME

Dear God, thank You for all the
good helpers in my life. I know
they are serving You by helping
others. Show me how to be a
helper too. In Jesus' name. Amen.

## HAVE FUN TOGETHER AFTER NAP TIME

Gather four stuffed animals.
Act out the story. Make one
animal the hurt man. Have two
animals pass him by, imitating
the sounds from the story. Let
your child be the good helper
who takes the hurt animal
to the innkeeper, which is
the last animal. Talk about
how the man must have
felt when no one stopped
to help. How did it feel to
have someone stop and
help? Jesus gives us that
loving, safe feeling. He is our
best helper.

## THOUGHTS FOR GROWN-UPS

Have you read stories about people who act like the Good Samaritan? Sometimes the stories are dramatic, such as when someone saves a drowning victim. Other Good Samaritans attract less attention, perhaps spending time at Christmas working at a homeless shelter.

Once in a while we hear news about a kindness gone wrong. A man stops to help change a tire and is robbed. A doctor tries to save someone's life, but the individual dies and the doctor is sued. In a society that applauds good deeds but is also quick to find fault or to litigate, how can you and your child stay safe and provide help?

Teach your child to dial 911 in a real emergency. Help your child practice describing imaginary problems and saying your address slowly into a play phone. Show your child numerous safe and simple ways to help: hold a door for someone with an armful of groceries, let a car cut in front of you in traffic, smile and say thank you to a harried salesperson.

Let people who meet you see Jesus in your words and actions. Model His love, which will make the world a little kinder today—because of you!

## ACTING IN FAITH

Who in your world—perhaps as near as next door or as far away as a third-world country—needs your time and interest? Spend five minutes right now providing help in one small way. With Jesus, you will make a difference.

# God Made It All

---

## The First Four Days of Creation
### (Genesis 1:1–19)

Long ago there was nothing at all.
There were no pumpkins or kittens or bologna sandwiches.
 *Shake head sadly.*

There were no elephants or dandelions or people.
There was nothing at all.
 *Shake head sadly.*

But God was there. God created everything out of nothing at all.
 *Spread arms wide.*

When God started to make the world, there was only darkness.
 *Tightly close eyes. What can you see?*

God created light. God saw that the light was good.
 *Open eyes. What can you see?*

God separated water into the sky above and the sea below.
 *Raise hands toward the sky, then touch the ground.*

Then God formed dry land between the seas and lakes
and rivers. Now water stayed in place. God saw that the sky
and the land were good.
 *Nod head yes.*

God made the sun to shine during the day.
*Touch fingertips overhead.*

For nighttime, God made the moon.
Sometimes it looks big and round.
*Touch fingertips overhead.*

Sometimes it looks like a thin sliver.
*Crook one finger.*

God created each and every star to fill the sky with twinkling light.
God saw that the sun and the moon and the stars were good.
*Wiggle fingers overhead.*

The world was no longer dark and empty.
*Shake head no.*

God filled the world with light and love. It was all very good.
*Spread arms wide.*

## PRAY TOGETHER BEFORE NAP TIME

Dear God, what a wonderful world
You made. Thank You for the
warm sun and the silver moon
and all the twinkling stars.
In Jesus' name. Amen.

## HAVE FUN TOGETHER AFTER NAP TIME

Help your child find shadows on the wall
or on the sidewalk, in the sunshine
or in the moonlight. Can your
child outrun her shadow? Can
your child step on your shadow
and make it stay in one place? Shadows
remind us that God's love and light fill our lives.

## THOUGHTS FOR GROWN-UPS

Science fiction stories make it interesting to speculate on the fate of
the earth if our planet stopped spinning or if it collided with a meteor.
But we enjoy these stories knowing that God is in control of our universe. God created our world with balance and order and beauty.

As you talk about creation with your child, stress the fact that God
is in charge. Help your child respond in wonder while you explore your
world—watching an ant struggle with a crumb, crunching dry fall leaves,
seeing raindrops splash against the window.

## ACTING IN FAITH

Look out a window for five minutes. Then on any sheet of paper—
even a paper bag—use a few crayons to express your feelings about the
day God has made. Don't create a realistic picture, just scribble colors
that express how you feel as you enjoy God's creation.

# A Little Each Day

## Jesus Grows Up in Nazareth

### *(Luke 2:39–52)*

When Jesus was a little boy,
He did not wear blue jeans or eat pizza.
*Do you like pizza?*

He did not ride in an airplane or go to the zoo.
*Roar like a lion.*

But Jesus did do many of the same things you do.
*Point to yourself and nod head yes.*

Every day Jesus ate the good food that His mother, Mary,
cooked for Him.
*Say, "Mmmm." Rub tummy.*

Maybe Jesus helped Mary fill a big jug of water at the well.
*How would you carry a big jug of water?*

Jesus liked to visit Joseph's carpenter shop. Maybe
He liked to feel the smooth wood and hear Joseph sawing.
*Pretend to saw wood.*

Maybe Joseph taught Jesus how to use a hammer
and make things Himself.
  *Pound fists together.*

Jesus liked to visit the marketplace with His mother.
There He could see all kinds of fruits and vegetables for sale.
  *What do you buy at the grocery store?*

Jesus also saw jugs and robes and baskets
and rugs for sale. Maybe He even saw camels
that brought things from far away.
  *Shade eyes and look far away.*

Jesus lived by the Sea of Galilee. He could wiggle
His toes in the sand and watch fishermen sail off in their boats.
  *Can you wiggle your toes?*

Jesus probably went to school. He would have learned to read
and write and count.
  *Count to 10.*

Jesus' teachers taught Him God's Word. He listened to the
teachers and the other students and shared His ideas too.
  *Point to ears.*

At night Jesus looked up at the sky and saw the moon and
stars—the same moon and stars you see in the sky.
  *Raise arms and wiggle fingers.*

Mary and Joseph took Jesus to the big temple church in Jerusalem. He talked with the wise teachers and priests. They were amazed at all He knew.

*Gasp in surprise.*

Jesus grew a little each day. He ate and slept and learned, just like you do.

*Point to yourself. Say, "I am growing too!"*

## PRAY TOGETHER BEFORE NAP TIME

Dear God, thank You for helping
  me grow in Your love. Help me to
  grow a little stronger and kinder
  each day. In Jesus' name. Amen.

## HAVE FUN TOGETHER AFTER NAP TIME

Use a pencil to mark your child's height on the inside of a door. Together, look at snapshots or a videotape of your child as a baby. Discuss things that your child can do now that he or she couldn't do as a baby. Record your child speaking or singing a favorite song. Add to the tape as your child grows.

## THOUGHTS FOR GROWN-UPS

How fast is your child growing right now? Is this an easy, enjoyable time or one of challenge and difficulty?

The enjoyment you get from raising your child may have less to do with the age of your child and more to do with your expectations. If your child is not measuring up, you may be looking for control and behaviors that aren't possible right now. Have patience with your child. Even Jesus grew up just a little bit each day! There is nothing your child will experience—from big barking dogs to overly stimulating birthday parties—that Jesus cannot understand.

You are in the process of growing too. You did not suddenly become a parenting expert the day your child was born! Each day brings new parenting challenges and decisions. Be patient with yourself. Think how lovingly Jesus treated children and how quickly He helped parents. There is nothing you will experience—from feeling irritated to worrying to quiet gratitude—that Jesus cannot understand.

As you read about and discuss parenting advice, let the love of Jesus be your guide in choosing what is right for you and your child.

## ACTING IN FAITH

Take five minutes to write about an unhappy childhood memory. Then imagine Jesus entering the scene to stop hurtful actions or give you the strength and support you need. Write a new ending to the incident with Jesus in the midst of the action.

# Who's on the Roof?

*(Mark 2:1–12)*

Healing the Man Who Came through the Roof

Once a man had four good friends.
   *Hold up four fingers.*

The man was crippled. He could not walk.
   *Shake head sadly.*

The man was sad that he could not walk.
He was glad that he had four good friends to help him.
   *Hold up four fingers.*

One day the friends heard that Jesus was coming to town.
They knew Jesus could make sick people well.
Maybe Jesus would heal their friend!
   *Clap hands in excitement.*

Each man took one corner of their friend's sleeping mat.
They carried him to the house where Jesus was.
   *Help hold the corners of a blanket or towel.*

So many people were crowded into the house that the four
friends could not get the man through the door.
   *Shake head sadly.*

The four friends whispered and pointed to the roof of the house.
   *Point to roof.*

The men carried their friend to the top of the house.
   *Raise hands above head.*

Carefully they made a hole in the roof and peeked down at Jesus.
*Shade eyes and look down.*

Jesus looked up to see a man on a mat being lowered into the room. On the roof were four good friends who believed Jesus could heal the man.
*Point up in surprise.*

Jesus looked kindly at the man. He said, "I forgive your sins."
*Stretch out arms in a helping gesture.*

Then Jesus said, "Pick up your mat and walk."
*Raise palms as if lifting a mat.*

The man picked up his mat and walked!
*Pat hands on knees.*

Happily, the four men and their friend walked home.
*Hold up five fingers.*

## PRAY TOGETHER BEFORE NAP TIME

Dear God, thank You for good friends who help me. Show me how to be a good friend to others. In Jesus' name. Amen.

## HAVE FUN TOGETHER AFTER NAP TIME

Use a baby blanket or a towel for the mat and a doll or a stuffed animal for the man who could not walk. You and your child can carry the blanket just as the friends did in the story. Then run and jump together as you thank God for giving you strong legs.

## THOUGHTS FOR GROWN-UPS

Has *why?* become your child's favorite question? You may find yourself asking God that same question, particularly when friends and loved ones become ill or experience trouble.

God does not mind being asked *why?* He hears not only the question, but the pain and sorrow, the desperation and disillusionment that prompt it. Through the death of His Son, God forgives our questioning and doubts. He promises to fill us with His strength and bring good from every experience, no matter how troubling.

You will not see the full scope of God's plans on this side of heaven. You are assured of His loving presence throughout difficult times and His willingness to listen and to send supportive people into your life. He will fill you with the love and care you need to respond when a friend or family member asks, "Why?"

## ACTING IN FAITH

Write a short note or send a get-well card to someone who needs cheering up and strength. Include a Bible verse you find helpful in troubling times.

# What's for Dinner, Moses?

## Manna and Water in the Wilderness

### *(Exodus 16:4–5; 17:3–6)*

Long ago God's people had to work hard as slaves in Egypt.
  *Wipe brow and say, "Whew!"*

God chose Moses to lead His people to a new land
where they would be safe and happy.
The people walked through the desert for a long, long time.
  *Pat hands on knees.*

The people could not find any water in the desert. They were thirsty.
  *Touch fingers to throat.*

"Does God want us to be thirsty, Moses?" the people asked.
"We will die without water."
  *Hold palms up in questioning gesture.*

God told Moses to hit a rock with his stick.
  *Clap hands.*

The people watched as Moses hit the rock.
  *Point to eyes.*

Water flowed out of the rock where Moses hit it.
It was clear and clean and ready to drink.
The people drank and drank.
  *Pretend to take a big drink.*

The people got hungry too. They missed
the good food they had in Egypt.
  *Rub tummy.*

God said, "I will send bread from heaven for the people. They should get up early in the morning to gather it."

*Yawn. Do you like to get up early?*

God covered the ground with white bread.

*Pat the ground.*

The bread was called *manna*. Each day the people collected enough to eat.

*Pretend to hold handfuls of manna.*

God took good care of His people. He gives you the things you need too.

*Nod head yes.*

## PRAY TOGETHER BEFORE NAP TIME

Dear God, thank You for giving me the food I need every day. Help me to share with others. In Jesus' name. Amen.

## HAVE FUN TOGETHER AFTER NAP TIME

Sing the words on the next page with your child to the tune of "Mary Had a Little Lamb":

God will give us food to eat,
Food to eat, food to eat.
God will give us food to eat.
Thank You, thank You, God.

As you go through the day, sing the song often, replacing the words "food to eat" with other blessings: clothes to wear, toys to share, friends to love, etc.

## THOUGHTS FOR GROWN-UPS

Do you ever feel that you've reached the bottom of your resources, whether financial, emotional, or physical? In these times, perseverance, relying on "good luck," and "pulling ourselves up by our own bootstraps" are as futile as the Israelites' grumbling.

God works in every situation to give us exactly what we need. He may give you strength and courage to help you seek new solutions. He may provide you with colleagues and friends who lend a hand.

Big events and millions of small ones every day are gifts from God— blessings for us to enjoy.

## ACTING IN FAITH

Look at your calendar. Take five minutes to list blessings you enjoyed during the last week. Did you have enough money at the grocery store? Did you drive to school and back without an accident? Did you get a hug from someone you love? God is continually blessing you!

# The Best Gift

## The Widow's Offering *(Luke 21:1–4)*

One day Jesus and His helpers watched people
bring their offerings to the temple.
*Shade eyes and pretend to watch people.*

Many of the people were rich.
They wore purple robes and fine sandals.
They had rings of gold and bags full of money.
*Pretend to hold large bags of money.*

Jesus and His helpers listened to the rich people
drop their bags of money into the offering boxes.
*Pretend to drop money into the offering box.*
*Say, "Clink, clink, clink!"*

The rich people looked around proudly, then went on their way.
*Pat hands on knees.*

Jesus saw a poor woman come to the temple.
She did not have fine clothes or nice sandals.
*Shade eyes and pretend to watch the woman.*

The woman carefully dropped two tiny coins into the offering box.
*Pretend to drop two coins. Say, "Plink, plink!"*

Jesus said to His friends, "Many people gave a lot of money
to the offering today, but they have much more money
at home for themselves."
*Pretend to hold large bags of money.*

Jesus said, "The woman put everything she had
in the offering box. Now she trusts that God will take care of her.
Truly hers was the best gift."

*Nod head yes.*

## PRAY TOGETHER BEFORE NAP TIME

Dear God, remind me that You
provide me with all I need to live
each day. Help me share what I have
with others. In Jesus' name. Amen.

## HAVE FUN TOGETHER AFTER NAP TIME

Draw simple faces on two paper plates.
One face represents a rich man; the
other represents the poor widow.
Act out the story, using a large
handful of coins for the rich
man's offering and two pennies
for the woman's offering. Talk
about how the woman might
have felt as she gave God all
she had. Plan the offering that
you will give to Jesus when you
go to church.

## THOUGHTS FOR GROWN-UPS

For some people, giving money to others is not an issue. Either they have plenty of money and don't miss what they give away or they have so little that sharing with others is not an option. More than likely, you fall somewhere in the middle—you have enough to make ends meet but sometimes give reluctantly, worrying that you might need that money. When we consider the widow who gave everything she had, we feel guilty about our own lack of faith when giving.

Money! Those who have it are both envied and suspected. Those who don't are pitied. And the lack of talk about it in your family may have left you wondering what is the "right" attitude, what is God's attitude, about money?

God's Word tells us "the love of money is a root of all kinds of evil" (1 Timothy 6:10). God asks that we love Him before anything we acquire with money. To love God most is to remember the gift of His Son, Jesus, who saved us not with gold or silver, but with His own precious blood. To love God most is to remember His care and blessings as we weigh financial decisions. Try giving a percentage to God off the top of your income, rather than waiting to see if there is anything left after bills. God will provide for all you need and bless you with much more.

## ACTING IN FAITH

Gather loose change from around the house. Check your purse and pockets, under sofa cushions, the top of the dresser, the kitchen drawers, and anyplace else coins might lurk. Don't count the money. Seal it in an envelope and give this with your next regular offering. Or donate the envelope the next time you are approached for a charity.

# What Happened to Joseph?

## Joseph and His Brothers
*(Genesis 37:3–4, 20–24; 45:4–11)*

When Joseph was a little boy, his father, Jacob,
bought him a beautiful new coat.
Joseph ran to show it to his brothers.
   *Quickly pat hands on knees.*

The brothers were jealous. They thought their father
loved Joseph more than he loved them.
   *Fold arms in front of chest. Make a mean face.*

The jealous brothers took Joseph's coat away
and sold him to traders going to Egypt.
They thought they would never see Joseph again.
   *Wave good-bye to Joseph.*

Joseph was afraid, but he knew that God
would take care of him.
   *Fold hands.*

God used Joseph to help the people of Egypt.
Their crops did not grow. Joseph helped the pharaoh
store food so the people had plenty to eat.
   *Rub tummy.*

Joseph's father and his brothers were hungry too.
Jacob sent Joseph's brothers to Egypt to get some food.
   *Point far away.*

When the brothers got to Egypt, they asked the important man helping the pharaoh to give them food. They did not recognize their brother Joseph!

*Shake head no.*

Joseph said, "I am your brother Joseph!"

*Point to yourself.*

Now the brothers were afraid. What would Joseph do to them?

*Raise hands in questioning gesture.*

Joseph said, "God has saved me and helped me do good for others. Now I can help you and my father. I forgive you for the wrong you did." Then the brothers all hugged and cheered.

*Hug each other. Shout, "Hurray!"*

The brothers brought their father to Egypt, and they lived happily with Joseph.

*Think of a time you have forgiven someone.*

**PRAY TOGETHER BEFORE NAP TIME**
Dear God, help me to forgive
others who hurt me. Help the
people in my family to share
Your love. In Jesus' name. Amen.

## HAVE FUN TOGETHER AFTER NAP TIME

Have your child decorate a brown paper grocery bag with crayons or markers. Use lots of different colors. Cut a hole in the bottom of the bag and slit the bag up the front. Cut an arm hole in each side. Let your child wear the bag like a coat. Talk about how you show love to family members.

## THOUGHTS FOR GROWN-UPS

Why do some people act the way they do? Are they just mean and evil? Maybe if we could understand their motives, it might be easier to forgive them.

Forgiving is not dependant on some special knowledge or understanding, though. God forgives us freely because His Son suffered the punishment for our sin and for the sins of those who hurt us. God will help us share that same kind of unconditional forgiveness with others.

Remember that forgiveness does not include judging on your part. God will do the judging and allow necessary consequences. He will also protect you in harmful situations and help you find the support you need. Ask God to cleanse your mind of memories of past hurts and live in true forgiveness.

## ACTING IN FAITH

Call someone who is struggling with the issue of forgiving or someone whom you need to forgive. Offer to pray that God will give you both the ability to forgive.

# Crashing Waves and Wild Wind

## Jesus Calms the Sea
### *(Luke 8:22–25)*

39

One day Jesus took a boat ride with His helpers.
He was so tired that He fell asleep.

*Rest head on hands.*

The waves were quiet,
and the night sky was filled with stars.
Jesus' helpers felt sleepy too.

*Sh-h-h-h. Let Jesus sleep.*

Then a little wind began
to blow, and a few raindrops
splashed into the boat.

*Wiggle fingers. Say, "Woo-oosh!"*

Jesus' helpers were fishermen.
They knew a storm might come, but they were not afraid.

*Shake head no.*

Suddenly the storm grew' worse,
but Jesus was still sleeping.

*Rest head on hands.*

The wind blew harder.
Rain poured into the boat.

*Wiggle fingers. Say, "WOO-OOSH!"*

Jesus' helpers held on to the sides of the boat as waves
splashed inside. Now they were afraid.

*Make a frightened face.*

The storm got worse. Jesus' helpers tried to scoop water
out of the boat. "We're going to sink!" they cried.
"Why doesn't Jesus help us?" But Jesus was still sleeping.
*Rest head on hands.*

The strong fishermen were very afraid. They woke Jesus and
cried, "The storm will kill us all! Help us, Jesus!"
*Cup hands around mouth. Say, "Help us, Jesus!"*

Jesus woke up. He shouted to the wind and the rain.
"Stop! Be still!"
*Hold hand up. Say, "Stop!"*

Suddenly the water was calm.
The clear sky was full of twinkling stars.
*Wiggle fingers overhead.*

Jesus' helpers were amazed that Jesus could stop the storm.
They praised and thanked God that Jesus was their friend.
*Fold hands.*


### PRAY TOGETHER BEFORE NAP TIME

Dear Jesus, what wonderful things
You can do! Thank You for helping me when I am afraid. Amen.

## HAVE FUN TOGETHER AFTER NAP TIME

Fold a sheet of paper in half. Let your child scribble wildly on one half to represent the storm. On the other half, draw the calm water and a boat. Help your child place star stickers in the sky. Write the name *Jesus* in big letters across both halves of the picture. He's the one who made the difference!

## THOUGHTS FOR GROWN-UPS

Have you ever driven through snow, rain, or fog so thick that you could not see the road ahead? In times like these, our senses and confidence desert us. In times like these, we realize how truly small and powerless we are.

It doesn't always take bad weather to make us feel powerless, though. A storm can come into our lives through the illness of a child, financial uncertainty, or marital problems.

If you are like me, prayer comes easily in stormy times. I tell God about my desperation and fear in heartfelt prayer. But God doesn't leave us when the storm is past and the sun shines again.

Jesus is present in your life in stormy and quiet times. He surrounds you with His love and care every day—no matter what the day may hold.

## ACTING IN FAITH

List all the strategies you use to calm yourself—praying, taking a relaxing bath, walking, singing, breathing deeply, remembering a happy time, writing about your feelings, etc. Add the heading: Jesus can calm any storm. Hang the list where you will see it often.

# Who's in That Bush?

## The Story of the Burning Bush

*(Exodus 3:1–4:16)*

Moses took care of sheep. He found grass
for them to eat and water to drink.
  *What do sheep say? Ba-a-a!*

Moses slowly walked the sheep across the
desert to a mountain covered with green grass.
  *Slowly pat hands on knees.*

One day, as Moses was watching the sheep,
he saw a bush burning with fire.
  *Shade eyes to look.*

Moses saw that the bush was on fire, but it didn't burn up.
What kind of strange thing was this?
  *Raise palms in questioning gesture.*

Moses walked over to look at the bush.
  *Pat hands on knees.*

Then something very exciting happened.
Moses heard God's voice talking to him from the bush!
  *Cup hands around ears.*
  *How do you look when you are surprised?*

God told Moses to lead His people away from the mean pharaoh
in Egypt and take them to a new home.
  *Point far away.*

Moses said, "I won't know what to say."
*Shake head no.*

God said, "I will tell you what to say.
Now go!"
*Point far away.*

Moses said, "What if the people ask me Your name?"
*Raise palms in questioning gesture.*

God said, "Tell the people that 'I AM' sent you. Now go!"
*Point far away.*

God's name is "I AM" because He always was and is and always will be. God was there to help Moses, and He is here to help us today.
*Nod head yes.*

## PRAY TOGETHER BEFORE NAP TIME

Dear God, remind me that You
  can save me from any trouble.
  Help me always to follow You gladly.
  In Jesus' name. Amen.

Play a hidden voice game. Let your child see you hide behind a chair. Then give your child instructions from your hiding place: Jump up and down. Clap your hands. Give me a hug. Change places so your child can be the hidden voice and give you instructions. Tell your child that God speaks to us when we hear His Word.

## THOUGHTS FOR GROWN-UPS

Do your days run together so you find yourself saying, "I can't believe it is already autumn?" or "Where did the winter go?" Are you able to make time in your harried schedule to hear the voice of God? God knows you have a lot to do, but God also has a plan for your life—a bigger plan than just surviving each day and getting up to do it all again tomorrow.

If you are uneasy about your daily frantic pace and feel "something is missing," take time to hear God's voice. Leave some tasks undone and quietly read His Word. Make worshiping and communing at His altar a priority. God will speak clearly to you in His Word, letting you know that He will help you live out the plan He has for you.

## ACTING IN FAITH

Go to your favorite place to relax. Read a chapter from God's Word and listen to what He tells you. Write an especially meaningful verse on a small sheet of paper and keep it in your wallet as a reminder of God's will in your life.

# Breakfast Is Ready!

## Jesus Meets Peter on the Beach

*(John 21:1–17)*

Jesus died on the cross to take our sins away.
*Make cross with two fingers.*

Then Jesus came alive again!
*Raise hands in surprise.*

One night, after Jesus came alive, Peter and his friends
went fishing. They rowed their boat out on the water.
*Cup hands to form a boat.*

They fished and fished all night, but Peter and his friends didn't
catch anything.
*Shake head no.*

In the morning, a man stood on the beach and called to them.
*Wave hand in greeting.*

The man told the fishermen to throw their net on the other side
of the boat. When they did, they caught many fish!
*Hold up 10 fingers.*
*Say, "They caught more than that!"*

Then Peter knew the man on the beach was Jesus.
*Clap hands in surprise.*

Peter jumped out of the boat.
  *Make a "splash"!*

Peter swam to the beach to see Jesus.
  *Make swimming motion.*

Jesus cooked some fish and made breakfast for His friends.
  *Rub tummy.*

Jesus asked, "Peter, do you love Me?"
  *Raise palms in questioning gesture.*

Peter said, "Yes, Jesus. You know I love You."
  *Nod head yes.*

Jesus said, "Tell all of My friends about My love."
  *Hug yourself.*

Three times Jesus asked Peter to take care of His friends,
and three times Peter promised that he would.
  *Hold up three fingers.*

Jesus told Peter that He had forgiven Him for the things he had
done wrong. Jesus told Peter that He wanted him to be His helper.
  *Nod head yes.*

## PRAY TOGETHER BEFORE NAP TIME

Jesus, I'm glad You are alive!
  Help me to tell everyone about
  Your love. Amen.

49

## HAVE FUN TOGETHER AFTER NAP TIME

Cut simple fish shapes from scraps of paper. Let your child sit on a chair and dangle a string toward the floor. Tape one of the fish to the end of the string each time your child lets it down. Talk about how excited the disciples must have been to see their friend Jesus again. Decide whom you can tell about Jesus.

## THOUGHTS FOR GROWN-UPS

Do you sometimes feel like a failure in your faith life? Are there times when your words and actions have denied Christ, just as Peter did outside the judgment hall?

Don't despair. We can walk away from God, but He never walks away from us. Jesus speaks to you just as lovingly as He did to Peter. He tells you to feed His lambs, just as He told Peter. Jesus asks you to follow Him, to care for the people He loves, to rejoice in the forgiveness He won for you. How will you share your faith today?

## ACTING IN FAITH

Write "Jesus goes with me on life's journey" on a small sheet of paper. Tape the paper to the dashboard of your car. As you drive, ask Jesus to show you how to feed His lambs who gather around you.

# Moving Again!

## Abraham and Sarah Move to a New Land

*(Genesis 12:1–5)*

Abraham had a tent and many goats and cows and sheep.
*What do cows and sheep say?*

Abraham's wife, Sarah, had fine clothes and many nice things.
*Rub hands together and smile.*

One day, God spoke to Abraham. God said, "Go from this place to a land I will show you. There you will live and be happy."
*Point far away.*

God said, "I will bless you, and, through you, all people on earth will be blessed."
*Spread arms wide.*

Abraham looked at his wife, Sarah, and at his home and all his animals.
*Shade eyes and look around.*

Abraham folded up his tent and rounded up all his goats and cattle and sheep.
*What do cows and sheep say?*

Abraham and Sarah packed their things and set out for the land God would show them.
*Pat hands on knees.*

God led Abraham and Sarah to a beautiful new home.
*Spread arms wide and smile.*

God kept His promise to bless all people through Abraham's family. Many years later, God sent His own Son, Jesus, to be born as a relative of Abraham.

*Rock a baby.*

## PRAY TOGETHER BEFORE NAP TIME

> Dear God, I am so glad You are
> with me, even when I move from
> place to place. Be with me wher-
> ever I go. In Jesus' name. Amen.

## HAVE FUN TOGETHER AFTER NAP TIME

Show your child a picture of a friend or relative that you don't see often. Talk about how God cares for that person, just as He cares for you. Pretend to talk with that person on a play phone. Then make a real phone call to this person. Let your child say, "Jesus loves you."

## THOUGHTS FOR GROWN-UPS

"Geographic mobility" is not new. Abraham and Sarah knew that. It is rare for someone today to live their entire life in one location. Each move—or life change—brings feelings of being uprooted and unsettled. The question "Where shall I put the Christmas tree in this house?" is one you would like to answer as few times as possible.

If you moved tomorrow, what things would need to go with you? What would you really miss? What could not be replaced? You may think of family heirlooms, photo albums, or childhood treasures.

Make your faith in God the first necessity you take with you on your life's journey. He will lead you always, even to your final home with Him in heaven.

## ACTING IN FAITH

Call your church office to get the name of a new member who just moved to your town. Call that person or drop them a note, welcoming them and offering to help them in any way you can. Some ideas include: finding a dentist, providing information about Bible studies and church services, offering to baby-sit. God will bless that newcomer through your actions.

# Come Meet Jesus

## Jesus Blesses the Children
### *(Mark 10:13–16)*

Everyone in town was very excited. Jesus was coming!
*Clap hands.*

Mothers wrapped their babies in warm blankets.
*Rock a baby.*

The mothers gathered all their little children and ran to see Jesus.
*Quickly pat hands on knees.*

The mothers wanted Jesus to bless their children.
*Clap hands. Say, "What a good idea!"*

The mothers tried to bring their children close to Jesus.
*Slowly pat hands on knees.*

The disciples said, "Stop!"
*Hold up one hand.*

The disciples said Jesus was too busy to see the children.
*Shake head sadly.*

Then the mothers and children heard the kind voice of Jesus Himself. "Bring the children to Me," He said. "God's kingdom belongs to them."
*Reach out in gathering motion.*

The children ran happily to Jesus.
*Quickly pat hands on knees.*

Mothers put their babies in Jesus' arms.
*Rock a baby.*

Jesus blessed the children and told them that He loved them. *Hug yourself.*

## PRAY TOGETHER BEFORE NAP TIME

Dear God, thank You for making me Your child. I am glad You keep me close to You. In Jesus' name. Amen.

## HAVE FUN TOGETHER AFTER NAP TIME

Make this a hugging day. Write the words "Hug me!" on circles of paper, and decorate them with markers or stickers. Pin the circles on yourself and on your child. When either of you needs a hug, point to the circle and say, "Hug me!" Save your circles to wear on grumpy days or to share with other family members who may need hugs too!

## THOUGHTS FOR GROWN-UPS

It is not always easy to love your child. Differing personalities and temperaments can make your child a delight one minute, a grouch the next. Your child's actions might remind you of feelings and experiences—some good, some bad—you had as a child. These memories also will color how you relate to your child.

It is human nature to find your child appealing at some times and less so at others. It is Christlike to accept your child with loving forgiveness at all times.

Show your child how to love other children, even ones who seem unlovable at times. Jesus loves all people, especially the unlovable.

## ACTING IN FAITH

Think through your week with your child. What behaviors and attitudes frustrated you? What are your greatest challenges in sharing unconditional love with your child? Bring these concerns to Jesus, and ask His blessing on all your interactions.

# Cheetahs and Turtles and Duckbill Platypuses

## Noah's Ark
*(Genesis 6:11–7:5; 9:8–13)*

One day God told Noah to build a big boat.
*Spread arms wide.*

Noah looked all around.
He didn't see an ocean or lake or river to sail a boat.
*Shade eyes and look around.*

God said, "I will make it rain and rain
until all the land is covered with water."
*Wiggle fingers for rain.*

God would keep Noah safe on the big boat.
Noah sawed the wood.
*Pretend to saw.*

Every day he hammered and worked to build the big boat.
*Make hammering motion.*

God told Noah to take two animals of every kind on the boat.
*Hold up two fingers.*

Noah brought fast animals like cheetahs and rabbits.
*Zoom!*

He brought big animals
like elephants and hippos.
*Spread arms wide.*

He brought funny animals
like duckbill platypuses.
*Can you say "duckbill platypus"?*

Noah brought little animals like mice and spiders.
*Walk fingers up arm.*
*Say, "Creepy, creepy, crawly."*

Noah brought very slow animals like turtles.
*Slowly walk fingers up arm.*

When Noah and his family
and all the animals were safe on the boat,
God closed the door with a bang.
*Clap!*

Then God sent the rain. It rained and rained until there was no
land left. All Noah could see was water.
*Wiggle fingers for rain.*

Inside the boat, Noah's family and all the animals were warm
and dry. God kept them safe.
*Cup hands to make a boat.*
*Make a rocking motion.*

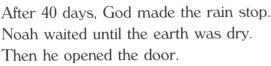

After 40 days, God made the rain stop.
Noah waited until the earth was dry.
Then he opened the door.
Off ran the cheetahs and the rabbits.
*Zoom!*

Off marched the big elephants and hippos.
*Spread arms wide.*

Off waddled the funny duckbill platypuses.
*Wave good-bye to the duckbill platypuses.*

Off scurried the little animals like the mice and spiders.
*Run fingers down arm. Say, "Creepy, creepy, crawly."*

Off crawled the slow the turtles.
*Slowly walk fingers down arm.*

Noah thanked God for keeping all of them safe.
*Fold hands.*

God put a rainbow in the sky as a promise that
He would never again cover the earth with water.
*Trace a rainbow shape in the air.*

## PRAY TOGETHER BEFORE NAP TIME

Dear God, thank You for saving
Noah's family and all the animals.
I will remember Your promise each
time I see a rainbow.
In Jesus' name. Amen.

## HAVE FUN TOGETHER AFTER NAP TIME

Change into swimsuits for a mid-day bath. Use chenille wires to make Noah and different animals. Fill the tub (or an outdoor pool) with water. Use a plastic container for the ark. Have fun splashing wildly while the rain falls. Then drain the tub or empty the pool to make dry land appear.

## THOUGHTS FOR GROWN-UPS

At the time of the flood, Noah and his family were the only people on earth who remained faithful to God. If you and your family had lived at that time, would you have made it into the ark?

Guilt weighs us down when we lose our temper with our child, fail to report getting too much change at the drive-through window, or hurt a friend's reputation with gossip. Then the ark, and God's forgiveness, seem far away.

Don't worry. You would make it onto the ark with time to spare. Not because of your goodness, but because Jesus was born to fulfill the demands that God makes of us. Jesus died so our shortcomings would be forgiven. We are a member of Noah's family on the ark, not for our own sake, but because of Jesus.

## ACTING IN FAITH

List things you have worried about—and continue to worry about—this week. Ask God to take your worries away. Be assured that He can save you from overwhelming worries as easily as from raging water. Throw the list away and praise God for keeping you close to Him.

# More than Enough Food

## Jesus Feeds 5,000 People
### (Mark 6:35-44)

Jesus told everyone about God's love.
*Hug yourself. Say, "God loves you!"*

One day more than 5,000 people came to hear Jesus talk.
They stayed and listened to Him all day.
*Point to ears.*

As the sun was going down, the disciples told Jesus to send
the people away to get food.
*Rub tummy.*

Jesus said, "You give them something to eat."
*Point to each other.*

The disciples found a little food—five loaves of bread
and two little fish.
*Hold up seven fingers.*

That would be enough to feed one person,
not more than 5,000 people.
*Hold up one finger.*

Jesus took the little bit of food and blessed it.
*Fold hands.*

Jesus said to the disciples, "Feed the people." So the disciples gave food to a few people, but there still was bread and fish left.
*Cup hands. Look at them in surprise.*

They gave food to more people,
and there still was bread and fish left.
*Move hands farther apart.*

They gave food to many people,
but there was still bread and fish left.
*Spread hands farther apart.*

Even after all the people had eaten all the bread and fish they wanted, there still were pieces left.
*Spread arms wide.*

Jesus had fed all the people with a little bit of food. The people praised God.
*What food do you want to thank Jesus for?*

## PRAY TOGETHER BEFORE NAP TIME

Dear Jesus, how happy I am that
You can do such amazing things!
Give me faith to know that You
always will care for me. Amen.

## HAVE FUN TOGETHER AFTER NAP TIME

Help your child use cookie cutters to cut shapes from bread, then spread them with peanut butter or cheese. Put them on a plate and share them with a neighbor as an afternoon snack. Talk with your child about how it feels to share.

## THOUGHTS FOR GROWN-UPS

What is enough? In a world driven by "faster," "more powerful," "bigger and better," is there any limit to the material possessions one wants?

In a land where even the least affluent have more than people in many parts of the world, it is easy to ignore the needs of those around us. When one considers people who are starving, homeless, lacking medical care, even lacking the saving news of the Gospel, it seems impossible to make a dent in the world's sorrow. But the God who turned a little boy's lunch into a meal for thousands will make much out of your small gifts. When you help in a soup kitchen, donate food and clothes to a shelter, give your offering to spread the proclamation of the Gospel, and offer God's comfort to a hurting friend, God will work mightily through your actions.

## ACTING IN FAITH

Look in your kitchen cupboards. If you have two packages of macaroni and cheese, put one in a grocery bag. Do the same with other canned goods and non-perishable items. When the bag is full, put it in the car. Take it to a food pantry the next time you go out.

# I Found It!

## The Story of the Lost Sheep
### (Luke 15:1–7)

Jesus told us stories about God's love.
  *Hug yourself. Say, "God wants you this close."*

One story is about a man who had 100 sheep. He counted them
every night.
  *How high can you count?*

One night, one little sheep was lost. The man left the other sheep
in the pen and went to took for the little lost sheep.
  *Shade eyes to look for the sheep.*

He looked on top of rocks.
  *Place one fist on top of the other.*

No sheep.
  *Shake head no.*

He looked under trees.
  *Hold arms out like branches.*

No sheep.
  *Shake head no.*

68

He looked behind bushes.
*Hold up fingers and look through them.*

Finally, the man found his little sheep.
*What do sheep say?*

The man carried the little sheep all the way home.
*Cradle sheep in arms.*

He gave a big party to celebrate that his lost sheep had been found.
*Shout, "Hurray!"*

God loves each of us the way the man cared for his sheep.
*Cradle sheep in arms.*

When we do something bad, we go away from God.
*Walk fingers on arm.*

But God forgives us and keeps us close to Him because He loves us.
*Hug someone you love.*

### PRAY TOGETHER BEFORE NAP TIME

Dear God, thank You for loving me
so much. Thank You for keeping
me close to You. In Jesus' name.
Amen.

## HAVE FUN TOGETHER AFTER NAP TIME

Play "Lost and Found" by hiding a cotton ball and letting your child find it. Make the hiding places obvious at first, then choose more challenging places. Talk about being lost and how it feels to be found and to find someone.

## THOUGHTS FOR GROWN-UPS

Have you ever been in a crowded place, only to be separated from those with whom you are walking? The feeling of apprehension grows as you strain for a glimpse of your companions. Can you recall the huge relief you felt when you were reunited? Imagine what it must feel like to be lost when you are only three feet tall.

Teach your child what to do if he or she becomes lost. Some ideas include: Ask a person in uniform, or someone who is working in a store, for help. Stand in one place and stay there until mom or dad finds you. Never threaten to leave your child in a public place, even if your child is moving slowly and you are in a hurry. Your child does not have the experience or the cognitive ability to understand that you are not serious when you say, "Well, good-bye. I'm leaving you." Pick your child up, even if you make a scene, and leave together.

Thank God for the many ways—His Word, His Supper, worship with family and friends—He uses to keep you close to Him.

## ACTING IN FAITH

Browse through your address book or Christmas card list. What friend do you still think about but don't communicate with on a regular basis? Pray for that person. Call or write a note, thanking God for your friendship and explaining that you don't want to lose touch.

Taking Care of God's World

# God Creates Plants, Animals, and People
*(Genesis 1:11–13; 20–31)*

Once there were no soft chicks or fuzzy dandelions.
God created everything that we can see and hear and touch.
*Point to eyes and ears.*

After God separated water and dry land,
He made plants grow on the land.
*Can you see a plant right now?*

God made cherry trees and grapevines.
*Wiggle fingers like growing vines.*

God made flowers that smelled sweet
and corn that grew and grew and grew.
*Reach arms higher and
higher and higher.*

God made grass to sit on
and roll in.
*Roll hands over and over.*

Everywhere God looked,
the plants were very good.
*Nod head yes.*

Then God made animals.
God made little animals,
like mice with long whiskers.
   *Tickle cheeks where whiskers grow.*

God made giraffes to look over tall trees.
   *Stretch neck and look up.*

God made animals with hard shells,
like turtles, and some with soft fur,
like bunnies.
   *Can you see an animal right now?*

Everywhere God looked,
the animals were very good.
   *Nod head yes.*

God was pleased with His wonderful world,
but He was still not finished.
   *Shake head no.*

God took a bit of dust and formed
the most wonderful thing of all.
   *Rub hands together.*

God created a man, then
He made a woman.
*Point to each other.*

God made the people perfectly
good, just like Himself.
*Nod head yes.*

The man and woman would
feed the cows and get milk from them.
They would water the peach trees
and pick the peaches.
*Pretend to drink and eat.*

The plants and animals would
provide food for the people.
In God's perfect world,
there was enough for everyone.
*Spread arms wide.*

God looked at His world.
God saw that everything was very good.
*Say, "It was good!"*

## PRAY TOGETHER BEFORE NAP TIME

Dear God, show me how to take
care of the animals and plants
and the wonderful world You have
made. In Jesus' name. Amen.

## HAVE FUN TOGETHER AFTER NAP TIME

Enjoy a touch-and-feel adventure.
While your child's eyes are closed,
carry him or her to a certain
object inside the house or outside—
a blanket, a tree, the grass. Ask
your child to identify the object
without looking. Talk about the
different ways we find out about
things in the world. Talk about
how we care for the plants and
animals in God's creation.

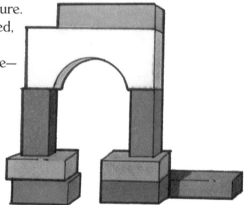

## THOUGHTS FOR GROWN-UPS

We are a nation, a generation, a world of consumers. We take and
take and take from the earth and from one another. It is easy to enjoy
the bounty of God's creation and ignore the responsibility He gave us
to care for His earth and His creatures.

It is usually easy to care for our children and the cat and the house-plants. It is harder to care for creation when it means giving up a convenience such as driving the car on every errand, recycling instead of throwing away, or sharing blessings with those less fortunate.

Look around you and thank God for all that you see. Ask Him to help you be a thoughtful consumer, a child of His who respects His creation.

## ACTING IN FAITH

Flip through the newspaper or a recent magazine. Find articles about people who help care for the earth, plants, or animals. Pray for their efforts. If possible, drop them a note that offers support for the work they do. Ask if there is a way you can make a donation or help in the effort.

# Teach Us How to Pray

Jesus Teaches
the Lord's Prayer
*(Matthew 7:9–13)*

One day Jesus' disciples said, "Lord, teach us to pray."
*Fold hands.*

Jesus said, "Our Father in heaven ..."
*Point up. Say, "You can call God 'Father' because
He loves and cares for you."*

"... Hallowed be Your name."
*Point to ears. Say, "God's name is special.
We use it when we pray to Him. God will always hear us."*

"Your kingdom come."
*Smile. Say, "God's kingdom is a happy place.
It is right here because Jesus is with us."*

"Your will be done on earth as it is in heaven."
*Clap hands. Say, "That's how fast God's angels in heaven
obey Him. He helps us to do His will too."*

"Give us today our daily bread."
*Rub tummy. Say, "God gives us everything we need every
day. What is your favorite food?"*

"Forgive us our sins as we forgive those who sin against us."
*Give someone a hug. Say, "God takes away the bad things
that we do. He helps us forgive others."*

"Do not lead us into temptation but deliver us from evil."
*Nod head yes. Say, "God gives only good things to us."*

"For the kingdom, the power, and the glory are Yours now and forever. Amen."

*Hug each other. Say, "God is with us right now and will keep us close to Himself always."*

Jesus talked to God whenever He was happy or sad or wanted to help someone.

*What would you like to pray about right now?*

## PRAY TOGETHER BEFORE NAP TIME

Dear Jesus, thank You for teaching me
Your beautiful prayer. Thank You for
hearing me every time I pray. Amen.

## HAVE FUN TOGETHER AFTER NAP TIME

Make a simple prayer book. Staple several sheets of paper together. On the first page write: God we thank You for ... Help your child think of things for which to thank God. Write one suggestion on each page. Ideas include Grandma, the sun, a favorite food, the dog. Let your child illustrate each page. Share the prayer book with the rest of your family, and use it as the basis for bedtime prayers this week.

## THOUGHTS FOR GROWN-UPS

Do you sometimes cringe when you see that your child has picked up one of your bad habits? It's amazing that you can say a thousand lovely words, but the one that slips out and you would rather not have repeated is the one your child mimics!

There is great power in modeling. Your child will accept being buckled into a seat belt if you are consistent about everyone in the family—including yourself—buckling up.

How much more important it is to model a life of prayer. You can teach simple prayers at mealtimes and bedtime. Let your child repeat a few words at a time until each prayer is mastered. Let your child see you at prayer and overhear you praying for him or her. Let your child hear you pray for strength when you are tempted, give thanks when you narrowly avoid an accident, and ask for forgiveness when you have said or done something hurtful.

Pray daily, asking God to bless your parenting and the child He has entrusted to your care.

## ACTING IN FAITH

Think about a situation that is troubling you. Which portion of the Lord's Prayer speaks to this situation? Pray that sentence and trust God to handle things.

# Jesus Is Alive!

Jesus Meets Mary in the Garden *(John 20:1–18)*

People who did not love Jesus killed Him on a cross.
*Make cross with two fingers.*

All Jesus' friends were sad.
*Make a sad face.*

For three days everyone was afraid and wanted to hide.
*Hide face in hands.*

On Sunday morning as the sun came up,
Mary walked to the garden where Jesus had been
put in the grave.
*Touch fingers overhead.*

The grave was empty! The stone closing it had been rolled away!
*Roll hands over each other.*

Mary ran to tell Peter and John what had happened.
*Quickly pat hands on knees.*

After Peter and John looked inside the grave and ran back
to the city, Mary stayed in the garden. She was crying.
*Make a sad face.*

Two angels said, "Don't be sad."
*Hold up two fingers.*

Then a man said, "Why are you crying?"
*Raise hands in questioning gesture.*

Mary thought it must be the man who took care of the garden. She asked him, "Where is Jesus?"

*Shake head sadly.*

But it wasn't the gardener—it was Jesus! He said, "Mary."

*Gasp in surprise.*

Mary was so happy to see Jesus.

*Smile. Point to lips.*

She ran to tell everyone the good news—Jesus is alive!

*Quickly pat hands on knees. Say, "Jesus is alive!"*


## PRAY TOGETHER BEFORE NAP TIME

Dear Jesus, I am so glad You rose
from the dead. I am glad You are
with me all the time. Amen.


## HAVE FUN TOGETHER AFTER NAP TIME

Use markers to write "Jesus is alive!" on a large sheet of paper. (Or use chalk to write it on the sidewalk.) Let your child add happy decorations. Talk about how wonderful it will be to hear Jesus say our names in heaven. Help your child "read" the message to other family members.

## THOUGHTS FOR GROWN-UPS

How often have you answered "in your heart" when your child asks where Jesus is? Ask Jesus to help you live out that answer today. Remembering this answer will help you speak a kind word to the harried clerk at the grocery store. It will help you refrain from honking your horn at the irritating driver. It will help you deal calmly with your child's temper tantrum.

Don't be too hard on yourself when you forget to respond to a situation in a Christlike manner. Remember that Christ looks at us with eyes filled with love. Even from the cross, He cried, "Father, forgive them!" He does the same for you.

## ACTING IN FAITH

Think about a friend or family member who seems to approach life with Christlike actions and attitudes. How do you feel when you are around that person? Ask Jesus to let His love shine through you today.

# Best Friends Forever

## Ruth and Naomi

*(The Book of Ruth)*

Ruth and Naomi were sad.
*Make a sad face.*

They were poor. It was hard to get food to eat.
*Rub tummy.*

Naomi said, "I am going to my home, Ruth."
*Point in one direction.*

"You can go back to your family."
*Point in opposite direction.*

Ruth said, "You are my friend, Naomi. I will go with you."
*Clasp hands together.*

Naomi and Ruth walked a long way to Naomi's old home.
*Pat hands on knees.*

It was still hard to get food. Ruth and Naomi were hungry.
*Rub tummy.*

Ruth went to a wheat field and picked up grain that the farmers
left behind.
*Pretend to gather stalks of wheat.*

The man who owned the field was named Boaz.
He told his workers to leave more grain for Ruth to pick up.
Now Ruth and Naomi had plenty of food!
*Happily rub tummy.*

Boaz asked Ruth to marry him.
*Pretend to put ring on finger. Say, "Hurray!"*

Soon Ruth had a baby boy.
*Rock a baby.*

Boaz and Ruth and Naomi knew that God loved them.
*Hug yourself.*

## PRAY TOGETHER BEFORE NAP TIME

Dear God, thank You for giving me
good friends just like Ruth and
Naomi were good friends. Help
me to be a good friend to others.
In Jesus' name. Amen.

## HAVE FUN TOGETHER AFTER NAP TIME

Help your child sing these words to the tune of
"Here We Go Round the Mulberry Bush."

I can sing about my friends,
All my friends, all my friends.
I can sing about my friends,
(*Name of friend*) is my friend.

As you go through the day, sing about other friends or people you
meet (for example, "The crossing guard is my friend.").

## THOUGHTS FOR GROWN-UPS

Ruth understood that love is not a romantic feeling. She displayed love in action through her loyalty and her assurance of "being there" for Naomi without question.

Where do you see that kind of loyal love in your life? Perhaps you know couples where one spouse is ill or disabled, yet the partner continues to display tender love. God seems to bless the healthy partner with superhuman strength to care for the one who needs help.

God fills each of us with the potential for that kind of love and loyalty. Ask God to help you give your child that kind of love and loyalty. Look for your child's loving actions and praise them. Let your spouse know that your relationship is a loving and loyal one. Verbal declarations of love are important, but it is the day-to-day actions of loyalty that bring love to life.

## ACTING IN FAITH

Who is your best friend? List the qualities that make that person a treasured friend. The next time you visit with that friend, thank him or her for sharing those qualities with you. Remember also that Jesus, your very best friend, is the reason you can share love with earthly friends.

# Little Birds and Pretty Flowers

The Lilies of the Field
*(Matthew 6:26–30)*

People loved to hear Jesus talk about God's love.
*Point to ears.*

One day Jesus wanted to tell the people that God
always would take good care of them.
Because God loved them, they didn't need
to worry about what they would eat or drink.
*Shake head no.*

Jesus pointed to some birds flying in the sky.
*Point to the sky.*

Jesus said, "Look at the birds. God cares for every little bird
in the sky. He makes sure they have plenty of food to eat."
*Flap arms.*

"God cares much more for you than
for all the little birds."
*Hug yourself.*

Then Jesus pointed to the flowers
growing wild in the fields.
"Look at the flowers," He said.
*Shade eyes and look far away.*
*Do you see flowers?*

"The flowers don't worry about finding
clothes to wear. God makes each flower beautiful."
*Cup hands. Pretend to sniff flowers.*

"God cares much more for you than for the flowers
that live only a short time."
*Hug yourself.*

We never have to worry about having the things we need.
*Shake head no.*

God always will take good care of us because He loves us.
*Hug each other.*

## PRAY TOGETHER BEFORE NAP TIME

Dear God, thank You for taking
care of the flowers and the birds.
Thank You for loving me much
more. In Jesus' name. Amen.

## HAVE FUN TOGETHER AFTER NAP TIME

Cut pictures of birds and flowers from magazines
and catalogs. Glue the pictures on a
paper lunch bag. Punch two holes
in the bottom of the bag, and
thread yarn or string through
the holes. Make a loop. Tape
crepe paper streamers or rib-
bons around the edge of the open
end of the bag. Hang the wind sock
where everyone can see it as a reminder of God's constant care.

How many truly "big events" have you experienced in your life? While we all have our share of red-letter days, much of life is made up of little experiences, day-to-day blessings that God sends to refresh you.

Sometimes stress over a major or minor problem consumes us with worry. In those times, it is easy to forget that God is in control. We don't take time to look at His reminders—the birds of the air or the lilies of the field—in the world around us.

How good it is to know that even when we don't take time to see the little blessings surrounding us, God has not stopped sending them! Remind yourself to look around yourself several times a day and thank God for the good things you enjoy. He continually blesses us with warm hugs, sunsets, fragrant trips to the bakery, crackling fires, and hot fudge on ice cream.

Even when times are so dark that you cannot enjoy these small pleasures, know that God is with you, filling you with the breath of life, holding you in arms that will never let you go, and saving a home in heaven for you because of the sacrifice of His Son.

## ACTING IN FAITH

Look around yourself without cleaning up or making any adjustments. Just appreciate what God has given you. Is the house a sea of toys? If you didn't have a child, the house would most likely be tidy. How much better it is to have a mess! Look for more blessings in everyday experiences.

# Only One?

## Jesus Heals Ten Men of Leprosy

*(Luke 17:11–19)*

Ten men were very sick.
*Hold up 10 fingers.*

The sick men could not stay at home.
They did not want their families to get sick too.
*Shake head no.*

One day the 10 men saw Jesus coming down the road.
*Shade eyes and look far away.*

They knew Jesus had made other people well.
"Maybe He would help them too.
*Nod head yes.*

The men called out to Jesus to help them.
*Wave arm. Say, "Jesus, have mercy on us."*

Jesus said, "Show yourselves to the priest in your village."
*Point far away.*

The men started walking to see the priest.
*Pat hands on knees.*

As they walked, they noticed that they were well!
*Smile.*

Nine of the men ran and ran.
They could not wait to get home.
*Quickly pat hands on knees.*

One man went back to see Jesus.
*Pat hands on knees.*

The man said, "Thank You, Jesus, for making me well!"
*What do you want to thank Jesus for?*

Jesus said, "There were 10 men who were sick."
*Hold up 10 fingers.*

"Only one has come back to say 'thank You.'"
*Hold up one finger.*

"Go home. Your faith has made you well."
*Quickly pat hands on knees.*

## PRAY TOGETHER BEFORE NAP TIME

Dear God, thank You for all the
good things You do for me. Help
me to thank others for their kindness too. In Jesus' name. Amen.

## HAVE FUN TOGETHER AFTER NAP TIME

Hide a small object behind your back. Give your child simple hints, such as: "It is yellow." "We eat it." "We peel off the skin and the fruit is inside." When your child guesses the correct answer, help him or her say thank You to God for the item. Then let your child hold something and give you clues. End each guessing game with a thank-You prayer.

## THOUGHTS FOR GROWN-UPS

"You can't play with any of your new toys until you have written all your thank-you notes." Oh, the drudgery of saying thank you! Even if you felt grateful for the gift, the seemingly artificial act of producing gratitude on the spot can spoil the feeling.

People tend to be extreme in their thanks or lack of it. Possibly you save up expressing gratitude until a really big event occurs, letting all the little kindnesses every day go by with only a grunt or without any recognition. Or you overuse the "what do you say for the nice present" words until they are meaningless, telling the bagger at the grocery store how big and strong he is for putting your items in a bag.

In what situations do you feel truly grateful? Thanking God for the blessings of the day is not so complicated. Unlike the aunt (or husband) who gives you a sweater you don't need or like, God knows you perfectly and gives you what you need to live each day. Recognizing God's blessings is the basis for gratitude that goes beyond words to generous and unselfish living.

## ACTING IN FAITH

Who needs a thank-you letter right now, not because that individual gave you a gift, but because he or she brings joy to your life? Could it be your parents, your spouse, or your children? How about God? Take five minutes right now to write what is in your heart.